MATH ATTACK!

Exploring Life Science with Math

EXPLORING LETHAL LIFE CYCLES WITH MATH

Robyn Hardyman

PowerKiDS press
New York

Published in 2017 by
The Rosen Publishing Group, Inc.
29 East 21st Street, New York, NY 10010

Cataloging-in-Publication Data
Names: Hardyman, Robyn.
Title: Exploring Lethal Life Cycles with Math / Robyn Hardyman.
Description: New York : PowerKids Press, 2017. | Series: Math attack: exploring life science with math | Includes index.
Identifiers: ISBN 9781499431339 (pbk.) | ISBN 9781499431353 (library bound) | ISBN 9781499431346 (6 pack)
Subjects: LCSH: Animal behavior--Juvenile literature. | Animal life cycles--Juvenile literature. | Animals--Adaptation--Juvenile literature. | Adaptation (Biology)--Juvenile literature.
Classification: LCC QL751.5 H349 2017 | DDC 591.56--dc23

Copyright © 2017 by The Rosen Publishing Group

Produced for Rosen by Calcium
Editors for Calcium: Sarah Eason and Jennifer Sanderson
Designers for Calcium: Paul Myerscough and Jennie Child
Picture researcher: Rachel Blount

Picture credits: Cover: Shutterstock: Kateryna Kon tl, Isabelle Kuehn br; Inside: Shutterstock: Chris Alcock 12, BellaNiko 5, 28t, BMJ 6, Hung Chung Chih 27, 29b, David Evison 8, Robby Fakhriannur 11, Fotovapl 18, GIRODJL 10, Teo Soon Haur 19, Willem Havenaar 24, 29t, Steve Heap 13, Kjersti Joergensen 9, Heiko Kiera 1, Lebendkulturen.de 14, 28b, Najmie Naharuddin 20, Jaime Pharr 22, Nicolas Primola 4, Punghi 15, Gordana Sermek 25, Mogens Trolle 26, Vladsilver 7, Volt Collection 23; Wikimedia Commons: Brett A. Goodman, Pieter T. J. Johnson 20–21b, Muhammad Mahdi Karim 16, Pjt56 17.

All rights reserved. No part of this book may be reproduced in any form without permission in writing from the publisher, except by a reviewer.

Manufactured in the United States of America
CPSIA Compliance Information: Batch #BW17PK: For Further Information contact Rosen Publishing, New York, New York at 1-800-237-9932.

CONTENTS

The Cycle of Life 4
Emperor Penguins 6
Sea Turtles 8
Deadly Mating Game 10
A Long Wait 12
Deadly Parasites 14
Cunning Wasps 16
Microscopic Life 18
Mutant Frogs 20
Plant Power 22
Patient Plants 24
Many Lives 26
Answers 28
Glossary 30
Further Reading 31
Index 32

The Cycle of Life

All living things have a life cycle: they are born, they grow, **reproduce**, and die. As they go through their life cycle, they change. For many living things, the young are similar to their parents but smaller. They grow until they become adults. Some animals, however, change dramatically between birth and adulthood.

Monarch Butterfly Life Cycle

adult — egg — larva — pupa — adult

Butterflies change completely during their life cycles, from egg to caterpillar, to **pupa**, to butterfly.

Survive or Die

There are many dangers involved in the process of reproducing. The natural world can be a tough place and, for many animals, it is a challenge to raise young and keep them safe from harm. Animals have developed many ways to give their offspring the best chance of making it to adulthood. These ways can be pretty nasty, and they can even be **lethal** for other animals.

Peaceful Plants

Plants are generally more peaceful in their life cycles. They often reproduce by creating seeds. These are carried away from the parent plant by the wind, by water, or when birds and other animals eat them and drop them in their waste. Once on the ground, the seeds can **germinate** and begin to grow into new plants. However, even plants face challenges in making sure they can create new **generations**. Some of them have developed smart ways of overcoming their challenges.

MORE THAN A NUMBER!

Cats can have 2 LITTERS per year. If the cat has 3 kittens in each litter, and each of those kittens has 2 litters a year, and those kittens do the same every year, after 5 years, that first cat will be responsible for more than 11,000 cats being born.

Trees, like these oaks, produce thousands of seeds each year that are carried to new places to germinate.

Emperor Penguins

At the South Pole in Antarctica, the winter is incredibly long. The sun hardly rises over the horizon for months on end, and temperatures are at least -40° Fahrenheit (-40° C). To add to the misery, the wind blows hard. It can reach speeds of 60 miles per hour (100 km/h), and blow for many days or weeks at a time. Emperor penguins, which are trying to rear their young, must face this hostile environment each day.

The male and female emperor penguins must rear their young in the harsh Antarctic.

Good Fathers

The Antarctic ice covers mostly land, not sea, but the sea holds the food that emperor penguins need to survive. It is impossible for both parents to feed at the same time while their young need to be reared, so the female lays a single, large egg. Standing on the ice, she passes it from her feet to the feet of the father. He tucks it under his thick skin into a special pouch. The female heads to the sea to feed, leaving the male to keep the egg warm through two months of the worst Antarctic weather. The male lives off the fat in his body. The egg must not touch the ground, or the chick inside will die from the cold.

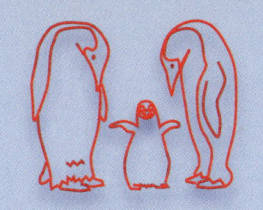

emperor penguins

Taking Turns

As the weather improves, the chicks hatch. The females return and, amazingly, they can find their mates among the colony of penguins. The females' bellies are full of food, which they regurgitate (spit out) and give to their chicks. The fathers head off to the sea for a well-earned meal. The chicks are still too small to survive on the ice. They must stay on their mothers' feet until they have gained enough weight and fat of their own.

MATH ATTACK!

The young chick stays warm inside the father's pouch.

A male emperor penguin weighs 80 pounds (36 kg) at the start of winter. When the female returns months later, he weighs 55 pounds (25 kg). How much weight has he lost? Use this calculation to help you solve the problem:

80 POUNDS − 55 POUNDS = ? POUNDS

Sea Turtles

Sea turtles are some of the bigger creatures in the ocean, and their life cycle is full of danger and drama.

Returning Home

Sea turtles are not born in the water. They hatch out of eggs on the beach. The adult females remember where they were born, and return to that very same beach when they are old enough to reproduce. This can be a long journey, even thousands of miles. They mate with males in the water near the shore, then swim onto the beach. They dig pits in the sand with their flippers, then lay 100 to 200 eggs in their pits. Some animals watch over their eggs until they hatch, but not the female sea turtle. She covers her eggs with sand and heads back to the ocean. Her job is done, and her offspring must look out for themselves.

The mother lays her eggs in a hole in the sand, covers them, and leaves for the ocean.

New Life

After two months, the eggs hatch. The baby turtles are tiny, but they must get to the ocean to find food. This is a very dangerous time for them. **Predators** such as birds and crabs are waiting to eat them. The turtles use their tiny flippers to crawl across the sand toward the water. Once in the water, they are still not safe from being eaten until they are more fully grown. Baby turtles can hold their breath for several hours, so they can find a safe place underwater and stay there for a while before coming to the surface to breathe.

MORE THAN A NUMBER!

When they hatch out of their eggs, baby sea turtles are just 2 inches (5 cm) long. However, they grow up to 5 feet (1.5 m) long and can weigh more than 700 pounds (300 kg).

The baby sea turtles make the most dangerous journey of their lives when they crawl to the ocean.

Deadly Mating Game

For some animals, finding a mate is one of the trickiest stages of the life cycle. Others struggle to protect their young until they reach adulthood. For one kind of insect, however, the act of mating is the greatest danger of all.

praying mantis

Powerful Praying Mantis

The praying mantis is a big insect, with large, strong front legs. These are bent up at an angle that makes the insect look like it is praying. These insects are very skillful at catching their **prey**, which are mostly smaller insects. Mantises have triangular-shaped heads and long necks they can turn, so they can see in all directions.

The praying mantis has powerful legs that strike out at a high speed to catch prey.

Males Beware!

When it comes to reproducing, the female praying mantis is more deadly than the male. She accepts a male as her mate, but then she quickly becomes violent towards him. As they are mating, or sometimes even before they mate, she starts chewing on his head. She will eventually eat it completely. This does not stop the male, though, who carries on mating. After the mating, the female then eats the rest of him. No one knows for sure why the female praying mantis turns on her mate in this deadly way. It may be a way of giving herself a good meal, so that she can pass the nourishment on to her young. She then lays her eggs, which later hatch into young called nymphs.

The mother praying mantis watches over her nymph.

MATH ATTACK!

The female praying mantis lays 100 to 200 eggs in a foamy pouch called an egg case. After a few weeks, they all hatch at once. If 3 mantises each lay 150 eggs, how many nymphs will there be? Use this calculation to help you solve the problem:

3 MANTISES X 150 EGGS = ? EGGS

A Long Wait

Life cycles can be long or short. For example, houseflies live for just four weeks. That is a long time compared with mayflies. Mayfly nymphs emerge from water, develop into adults, reproduce, and die, all within 24 hours. However, their complete life cycle does take longer. The eggs take a few weeks to hatch and the nymphs live underwater for several months.

The 17-year cicada waits a very long time for its short adult life to begin.

Life Cycle Stages

Most insects have a life cycle with several stages, just like mayflies. The females lay eggs, and they hatch into larvae. Some then have an inactive stage, called the pupa, before they change into adults. Others go straight from larva to adult, when they finally grow wings. In the eastern United States, however, there is one insect that takes an amazingly long time to reach the end of this cycle. You can guess why the 17-year cicada was given its name!

Female cicadas lay hundreds of eggs in cracks which they make in twigs and branches.

A Long Time

After they hatch from eggs, the nymphs of the 17-year cicada burrow down into the soil. That is where they stay for 17 long years. They drink the sticky juice called **sap** that the trees produce, as they slowly grow into adults. Finally, they emerge from the ground in huge numbers, buzzing loudly. They have just one month more to live. In that time they must mate and produce young for the cycle to begin again.

MORE THAN A NUMBER!

The 17-year cicada lives only in eastern North America – nowhere else in the world. It is the longest-living insect in North America. These cicadas emerge suddenly in late April or early May, sometimes with hundreds of thousands of insects per acre.

Deadly Parasites

Most animals have a life cycle that helps them stay alive long enough to reproduce to make sure their **species** continues. However, some creatures rely on other species to complete their life cycles. These animals have to infect members of a second species and live inside them. Creatures that infect other species in this way are called **parasites**. Species that are infected with parasites are called **hosts**.

Water fleas eat guinea worm larvae. Then they can be passed on to the host, which drinks the water.

Guinea Worm

The life cycle of the guinea worm is truly disgusting. The guinea worm larvae are very tiny. Water fleas, which live in water, like to eat guinea worm larvae. The larvae continue to live inside the fleas' bodies. When an animal (such as a human) drinks this water, the fleas and their parasites get into the animal's stomach. The stomach juices kill the fleas, but not the larvae. The larvae burrow out through the stomach lining into the second host animal's body. This is where they settle down, grow, and reproduce. The males then die, but the females move toward the host's skin where it is time for the next grizzly stage in the life cycle…

After a Year

After about a year living inside the host, a female guinea worm is around 2 to 3 feet (60 to 90 cm) long, and as thick as a strand of spaghetti. A blister appears on the host's leg or foot. One day, it bursts... and the head of the worm appears. This is so painful that the person or animal plunges its leg into water. This is just what the female guinea worm wants. As soon as the worm's body touches water, it releases thousands of new larvae into the water. Water fleas eat them, and so the cycle begins again.

Guinea worms infect people when they drink water containing water fleas in parts of Africa.

MATH ATTACK!

If 10 people are each infected by a guinea worm, and the worms each release 2,000 larvae into water, how many larvae will there be in the water? Use this calculation to help you solve the problem:

10 WORMS X 2,000 LARVAE = ? LARVAE

Cunning Wasps

There are many other parasites that use animals as hosts to complete their life cycles. Most of their stories are quite unpleasant, but the life cycles of the cockroach wasp is revolting.

Deadly Females

It is the female cockroach wasp that drives this deadly life cycle. She has a powerful stinger, which she uses to sting a cockroach, twice. The **venom** in her sting first **paralyzes** the front legs of the cockroach. This means it cannot use them to move. The second sting is to the head. This numbs its brain, so it will not try to escape. It is still alive, though. The wasp then eats part of the cockroach's **antennae**, and drags it off to her burrow.

The cockroach wasp has a metallic blue-green body, unlike more common wasps.

cockroach wasp

MORE THAN A NUMBER!

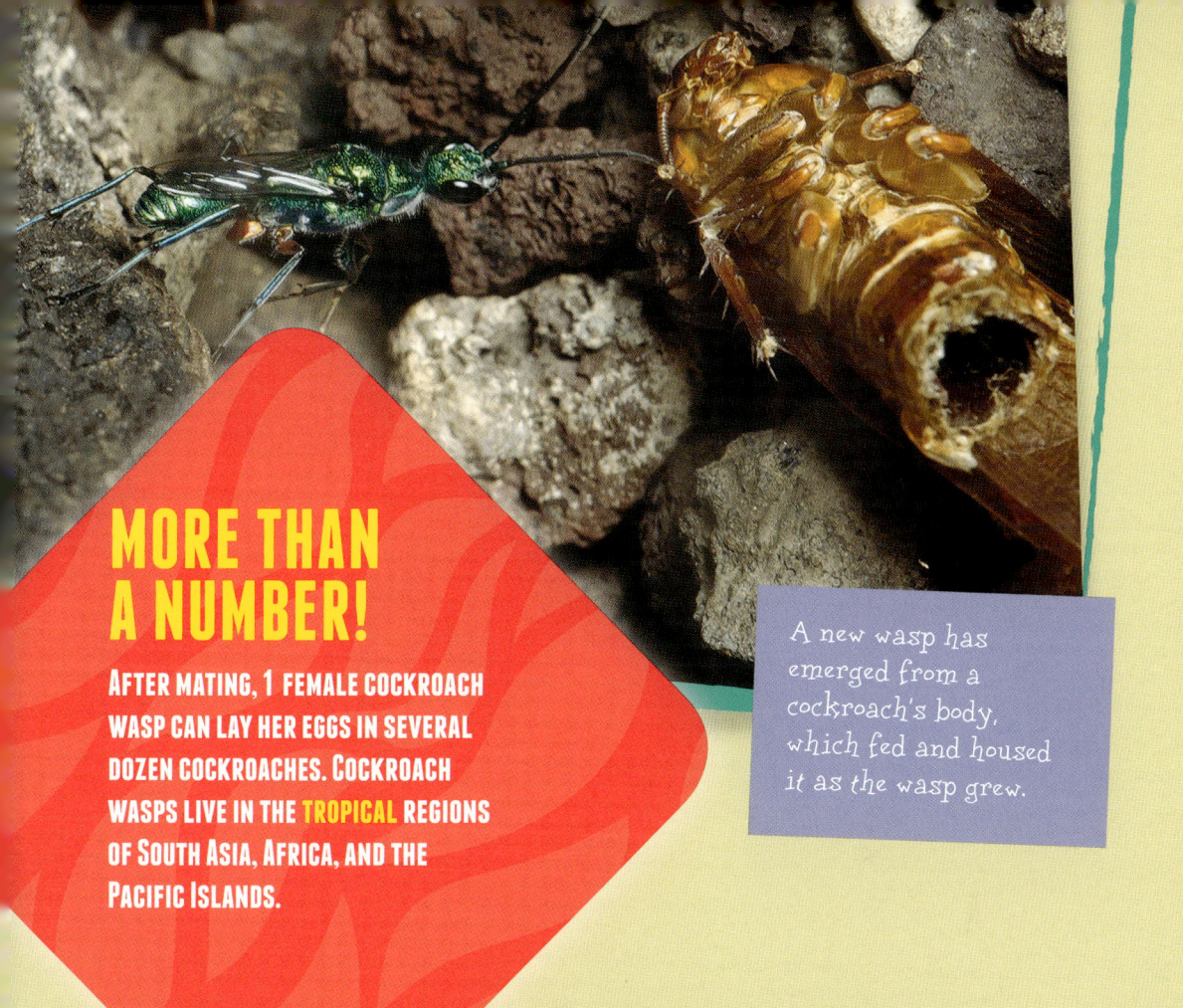

After mating, 1 female cockroach wasp can lay her eggs in several dozen cockroaches. Cockroach wasps live in the TROPICAL regions of South Asia, Africa, and the Pacific Islands.

A new wasp has emerged from a cockroach's body, which fed and housed it as the wasp grew.

Underground Horror

In the burrow, the wasp lays one egg inside the cockroach's body and buries the cockroach alive. After 3 days, the egg hatches, and a wasp larva appears. It has a good supply of food: the living cockroach. The parasite eats the cockroach's body over 2 weeks. It chooses which parts to eat first, to give the cockroach the best chance of staying alive because it is still needed for the next stage in the life cycle. The larva turns into a pupa inside the cockroach, and waits. Eventually, a grown wasp emerges from the pupa, and leaves the cockroach's body.

MICROSCOPIC LIFE

Some parasites are much smaller than wasps or worms. They are too small to see without a **microscope**. Their life cycles, however, are just as smart. One tiny parasite, called toxoplasma, can even influence the behavior of its hosts.

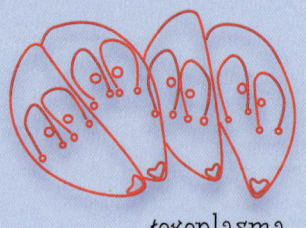

toxoplasma

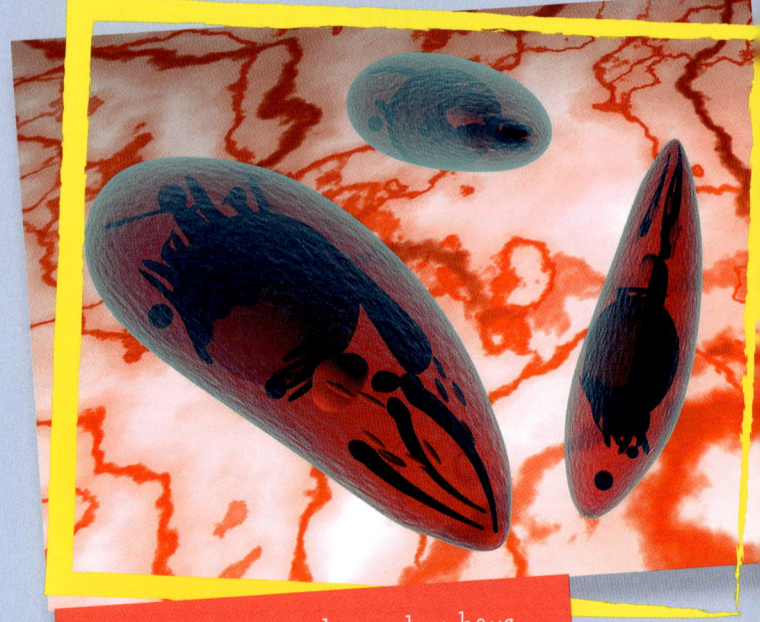

Most people never know they have toxoplasma in their blood.

Simple but Smart

Toxoplasma is a simple form of life called a **protozoa**. It may be simple, but it is certainly smart enough to spread itself around. It can infect any **warm-blooded** animal, such as a human. About one-third of all people in the world are infected with toxoplasma. Before you panic, it does not normally produce any unpleasant symptoms. When people eat meat that contains toxoplasma or touch cat feces, they become infected. That is because the toxoplasma really wants to live inside the body of a cat.

Cat Carriers

Toxoplasma can reproduce only inside the **digestive system** of a cat. The young are excreted in the cat's feces, so they must then get back into a cat to continue the species. Toxoplasma has a truly amazing way of doing this. It infects animals such as rats and mice. Normally, mice and rats know to stay well away from cats, because they are likely to be eaten. They sniff out cat urine, and keep away. Mice and rats with toxoplasma, however, behave differently. They are not afraid of cat urine. They may even seek it out. This makes them more likely to be caught and eaten by a cat. When the cats eat the rats or mice, the toxoplasma is back inside its ideal host. The toxoplasma actually affects the brains of the mice and rats, and changes their behavior.

MATH ATTACK!

If a cat eats 5 mice and each mouse contains 500 toxoplasma, how many toxoplasma will there be inside the cat's stomach? Use this calculation to help you solve the problem:

Cats and mice are important parts of the toxoplasma's life cycle.

5 MICE X 500 TOXOPLASMA = ? TOXOPLASMA

Mutant Frogs

There is another kind of parasite with an extraordinary life cycle. These creatures do not change the behavior of their host; instead they change its body. What is more, they need three different animal species to complete their fascinating life cycle.

Flatworms use three different species as hosts to complete their life cycle.

Flatworms

These parasites are flatworms. They live in water and, to complete their life cycle, they must spend time in the bodies of water birds called herons. Then they move on to snails, and finally, frogs. The adult flatworms live inside herons. When the herons' feces fall down into the water, the flatworm eggs go with it. In the water, snails eat the eggs. Inside the snails, the eggs hatch into mini parasites. They leave the snails and look for tadpoles, the early life stage of frogs. This is where the life cycle becomes really smart…

Tadpole Hosts

Tadpoles do not have legs but they are about to grow legs to become baby frogs. The mini parasites head for the spot where these legs are starting to grow, and burrow down. This makes the tadpole grow more legs than normal. It grows into a frog that is deformed. The flatworms want frogs to be deformed because a deformed frog is less likely to be able to escape from a hungry heron. They make easy prey. Herons eat flatworm-infested frogs, completing the flatworms' life cycle.

Frogs infected by flatworm parasites grow extra limbs.

MORE THAN A NUMBER!

The 5 species of frog most commonly infected by flatworm parasites are the green frog, Pacific chorus frog, northern leopard frog, northern red-legged frog, and Columbia spotted frog.

PLANT POWER

Animals aren't the only living things that can have lethal life cycles. Some plants have pretty scary ones, too. Some species of plants even kill and eat other living things to survive.

pitcher plants

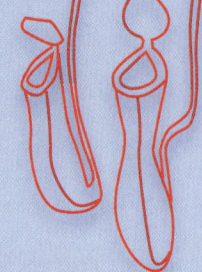

Meat Eaters

Most plants make their own food energy using sunlight and water, in a process called **photosynthesis**. Pitcher plants, however, are also carnivores, or meat eaters. They often grow in poor-quality soils, so they need the extra food they get from eating insects. They lure these insects in with their scent and colorful flowers. The flowers are shaped like pitchers, or jugs. They have steep, slippery sides. When an insect lands on the rim, it falls down inside and cannot get out. Down there, special liquids break down the insects' bodies so the plant can digest them.

Pitcher plant flowers and leaves grow directly out of the plant's thick roots underground.

Fire!

Many pitcher plants live in places where wildfires often break out. Most plants are killed when fires sweep through an area, but not the pitchers. They are left standing, and continue to grow. They can survive the blazes because they have large, fleshy roots underground that the fires do not destroy. Each year, new leaves and pitchers sprout directly from the roots. Pitchers really like the fires, because they clear away plants that would otherwise block out the sunlight they need for photosynthesis.

These pitcher plants grow in western Australia, where fires on open land are common.

MATH ATTACK!

At least 10 different kinds of pitcher plants grow in North America. There are about 100 different kinds growing around the world. How many more kinds of pitcher plants are there in the whole world than there are in North America? Use this calculation to help you solve the problem:

100 KINDS ÷ 10 KINDS = ? TIMES MORE KINDS OF PITCHER PLANTS IN THE WORLD

Patient Plants

Many plants grow in spring when the weather is warmer. They produce flowers in summer, and from these, the fruit develop. Inside the fruit are seeds. As the weather cools down, the seeds are spread, or dispersed, away from the plant. They settle on the ground and, in spring, new plants grow from them. For some plants, though, this is not quite how it works.

A Long Wait

Plants may live for just a few months, or for many years. Just as with animals, their life cycles can be long or short. However long they are, life cycles are always designed to suit the place where the plant lives. Plants want the very best chance of growing successfully and reproducing to make sure their species continues. That can mean a very long wait at some stages of the cycle. Poppies, for example, sometimes wait an incredibly long time. Their seeds can lie dormant in the ground for up to 80 years. This means they are not sprouting into new plants, but they are also not dead. The seeds usually grow when the ground is plowed or disturbed in other ways. Poppies often appear on battlefields, after the fighting has churned up the ground.

*Poppy seeds can lie **dormant** in a field for decades, until the ground is churned up.*

Speedy Plants

Other plants can reproduce much more quickly. Some develop places to store food underground, such as **bulbs**. These later develop into the following year's plants. Potatoes and daffodils do this, for example. Other plants are even speedier. They produce **runners**. These are shoots that grow sideways out from the main plant at ground level. As they touch the ground, they grow roots straightaway, so new plants can grow along the runners.

Strawberry plants reproduce by growing runners along the ground that take root and form new plants.

MORE THAN A NUMBER!

A SINGLE POPPY PLANT CAN PRODUCE UP TO 60,000 SEEDS. THAT MEANS THERE CAN BE HUNDREDS OF MILLIONS OF POPPY SEEDS IN A FIELD FULL OF POPPIES.

strawberry plant

25

MANY LIVES

We have seen how the animals and plants of the world have developed an amazing range of life cycles. In the tough natural world, every living thing must find ways to live long enough to reproduce, so their species can continue.

Getting On

Most animals, such as birds, fish, and **mammals**, have a simple life cycle with three stages: before birth, young, and adult. The young look like their parents but are smaller. Insects, though, change during their cycle and the young larvae do not look like the adults. Many species complete their life cycles all on their own, but parasites rely on other life-forms to survive and reproduce. They need a host, or even more than one, to live in during some part of their life cycle. The host suffers deformity, or even death, as a result.

In many mammal life cycles, the mother looks after her young until they can manage on their own.

Life Cycle Struggles

For a few animals, the odds are against them completing their life cycles successfully. The giant panda is one example. These large animals face big challenges to their survival. They eat only bamboo, which does not contain a lot of nourishment, so they need to eat a lot of it. The females can become pregnant on only a few days every year, which lowers their chances of having young. The young cubs are totally helpless, and cannot even crawl until they are three months old, so many do not survive. We are not helping the panda's chances, either, by cutting down the bamboo forests they need for food. This life cycle is most definitely under threat.

MATH ATTACK!

There are only about 1,000 giant pandas left in the wild. Special places have been created to try to breed more pandas. If people can breed 20 pandas every year, how many years will it be before there are 500 more pandas? Use this calculation to help you solve the problem:

500 PANDAS ÷ 20 PANDAS A YEAR = ? YEARS

The life cycle of the giant panda faces many natural challenges, as well as others we have created for them.

ANSWERS

Now that you have read many facts and figures about life cycles, try to learn more. It would be good to find out about the animals that live near you. Here are the answers to the Math Attack problems. How did you score?

PAGE 7:
80 POUNDS − 55 POUNDS = 25 POUNDS

PAGE 11:
3 MANTISES × 150 EGGS = 450 EGGS

PAGE 15:
10 WORMS × 2,000 LARVAE = 20,000 LARVAE

PAGE 19:

**5 MICE X
500 TOXOPLASMA
= 2,500 TOXOPLASMA**

PAGE 23:

**100 KINDS ÷ 10 KINDS = 10 TIMES MORE
KINDS OF PITCHER PLANTS IN THE WORLD**

PAGE 27:

**500 PANDAS ÷ 20 PANDAS A YEAR
= 25 YEARS**

GLOSSARY

antennae Long, thin stalks on a bug's head used for sensing.

bulbs Underground food stores made by plants.

digestive system The parts of the body used for digesting food.

dormant Living but not active.

generations All the people or animals born and living at about the same time.

germinate When a seed starts to develop into a new plant.

host The animal used by a parasite.

lethal Causing death.

litters The young born to mothers at one time.

mammals Animals that are usually hairy and feed their young with milk.

microscope An instrument used for making very small things look bigger.

paralyzes Removes the ability to move.

parasites Animals that live in or on other animals.

photosynthesis The process plants use to make their food from the energy in sunlight.

predators Animals that hunt other animals for food.

prey An animal that is killed by another animal.

protozoa A simple life-form.

pupa An inactive stage in the life cycle of an insect while its body is changing.

reproduce To have young, or offspring.

runners Stems that grow from a plant and put down roots.

sap A sticky juice that plants produce.

species A kind of living thing.

tropical The areas of the world close to the equator.

venom Poison.

warm-blooded Having blood that remains warm all the time.

Further Reading

Books

Amstutz, Lisa J. *Investigating Plant Life Cycles* (Searchlight Books: What Are Earth's Cycles?). Minneapolis, MN: Lerner Publishing Group, 2015.

Kalman, Bobbie and Robin Johnson. *The Lifecycle of an Emperor Penguin*. St. Catharines, ON: Crabtree, 2006.

Spilsbury, Louise. *Kill or Die: Extreme Life Cycles* (Extreme Biology). New York, NY: Gareth Stevens Publishing, 2015.

Websites

Due to the changing nature of Internet links, PowerKids Press has developed an online list of websites related to the subject of this book. This site is updated regularly. Please use this link to access the list: **www.powerkidslinks.com/ma/lifecycles**

INDEX

C
cicada, 12–13

E
egg, 6, 8–9, 11–13, 17, 20, 28
emperor penguins, 6–7

F
females, 6–8, 11–17, 27
flatworms, 20–21
frogs, 20–21

G
giant panda, 27, 29
guinea worm, 14–15

H
host, 14–16, 18–19, 21, 26

I
insect, 10, 12–14, 22, 26

L
larvae, 12, 14–15, 17, 26, 28

M
males, 6–8, 11, 14
mating, 10–11, 17
mayflies, 12

N
North America, 13, 23
nymphs, 11–13

P
parasites, 14, 16–18, 20–21, 26
photosynthesis, 22–23
plants, 5, 22–26, 29
praying mantis, 10–11
protozoa, 18
pupa, 12, 17

S
sea turtles, 8–9

T
toxoplasma, 18–19, 29

W
water fleas, 14–15